Mutant Musings on Tenderness

Bianca Laycock

BookLeaf Publishing

Presentation by *BookLeaf Publishing*

Web: www.bookleafpub.com

E-mail: info@bookleafpub.com

ISBN: 9789357445313

First edition 2022

DEDICATION

For Egg

PREFACE

This collection captures a moment in time, 21 days of September in lockdown. I wrote what was relevant to me in that moment - both figuratively and in reality - and this is the result. I'm not a trained poet, but I am an aspiring creative who needed an outlet. I hope these poems are as fun to read as they were to write.
- Bianca

Slugs

Once upon a time, in a harsher land than this
A monstrous single-footed creature roamed
A heart of obsidian
A soul of crushed glass
A hunger for power
The Earth shines where he touches
Showing where glory came from

He went to warn the cowards and tame the followers
His mucus mercenaries
For eons he reigned
A powerful nomad
Who made the world his home
Even today lived on
Through his descendants

Those who still conquer the world of tiny beasts
Living amongst us
Unsuspecting humans
A world that has always been theirs
One day we will know
The truth from whence we came

The Frog Duet

One bound away doth her skin glisten
No greater pond could she position
Her mighty nest of froglet babes
Nestled in reeds and grass blades

I stare, wholly in adoration
As she has captured the fair nation
Of my heart, though I must question
What team has her heart's possession?

Not any frog, as you're aware
May take the hand of one so fair
Not all frogs will it satisfy
To bed a lady, not a guy

Grass Hair

Grass is the leg hair
Of Mother Nature
A bit prickly
She hasn't shaved recently
In some places waxed off completely
She's living her truth

Maybe that is the reason why
Bare skin on grass
Is so refreshing
The leg hairs are connecting
At their annual family barbecue
I support it

Sometimes I take my legs
And place them on the grass
It's the least I can do
A simple thanks
For their faithful walking assistance

Abstraction

Abstraction is action
The act of making art
Not simply a picture
But the result
Of an event

Abstraction is distillation
Taking motifs and themes
To their limits
How far can we push away
From reality

Abstraction is absence
Leaving things out
Conspicuously
Showing what it cannot show
The picture of its own
Limitations

Universe

I am hoping
One day soon
I'll say I love you
To the moon
and back
And life will seem sweeter
Than before we ever kissed

Mutant Divine

If I stand on land in the sea
As all land tends to be
Will I be governed by man
Or by circumstance?

If governed by man
I would like to believe
Man hands the reigns
To the king of the seas

Any law that is broken
Is not fought with reason
But makes me most wanted
The next fishing season

As writhing limbs mimic
The turning of waves
I journey amongst them
Hope innocence saves

While the laws are unknown
To all those above water
Hints from travellers past
Help save me from slaughter

When days become years
I think I've succeeded
It’s time to come home
Where I am most needed

But if circumstance calls
And bad things befall
Who can I blame
But the fates?

Reality

It's alien to me
That I can't just
Paint myself to be
You
And have people believe it

Identity is arbitrary
So why can't I throw it away

Cows are the Silent Jury in the Trial of Mankind

Is it a poignant statement
Prophesying the fall of man
And the rise of cloven herbivores
Who judge our mockery
Of Mother Nature?

Or a taunt
From those we presume primitive
As they watch
From the sidelines?

Or perhaps insight
Into the nature of cattle
And similarities
To sheep
A comment on humanity
Foolishly docile?

Or most likely
Simply a phrase
Printed on a shirt
I wear as pyjamas

Red Sneakers

If I was a leopard with shoes
The people who stare I'd amuse
By acting a fool
While I try to be cool
Just like you when you get on the booze

Window to the Soul

The veil is lifted
An organza floodgate opened
Holding back not water
But emotion

Feelings indescribable
Swirling in the gap between our faces
Marbling the air
In a way only decipherable
By those versed in our brand
Of tenderness

A two-way connection
Between my eyes and yours
Without words we know
Your love for me
And my love for you
Is endless

Cafe Crisis

The time comes
They are waiting
I grasp
It slips away
A second attempt
Just as fruitless

Tucked into its bed
I cannot coax
The key to fortune
From whence it lies
Success eludes me

My nails long
Dexterity waning
Not yet a master
Far from it
Amateur

A gentle shove
A new tactic attempted
Pushing it from its cage
This escapade seems
Far from over
Embarrassing

Hark, an offer of assistance
A lady reaches yonder
To my purse
Retrieves my debit card
Her fingers unhampered
Finally, this transaction
Complete

Crunch

Crunch
Crunch
Footsteps on fresh snow
Cracking knuckles unsatisfyingly
Tearing a muscle
Eating cereal before it gets moist
Biting an ice cube with your molars
A dog cracking through cartilage
Crunch
Crunch
Crack

Which came first?

I lay in a hole of my own creation
Custom fit for my lonesome form
No need for sight
In these earthly depths
Anyone, the soil accepts

Never has my life required
The power of a mind stronger
Than that of a bug
As I slink beyond
Anywhere, I seek to wand

I sense a tussle amongst the dirt
Unnaturally twisting as never before
In my days amidst
This breath and being
Always, without eyes seeing

Thrust yonder to the surface over
By forces Godly in might
My pinkness accosted
The sun brings life
Alas, elemental strife

I rise at speeds unforetold
Clamped between the pincers
Of a creature feathered
Destined for the fated maw
Aptly, nature's law

Disappearing into the gullet
Is it a blessing or a curse
To be swallowed whole?
I thank the Earth
Anew, to undergo rebirth

Neigh ;)

A hoof scrapes
Kicking up the dust
Buzzing flies encourage
The flick of a mane
Neck twisting

The grounds crossed
In three bounds alone
All feet airborne
With a gallop
Fierce competition

Others watch on
The impressive athleticism
Seems strange to some
Especially at school
Horse girl

Frankie

O sweet car o mine
Sitting there in cream and black
With checked hats on your mirrors
And a dent in the back

Enemy of authority
When police park by your rear
Reverse to knock them down
Leave a motorbike smear

Upon your dash sits Gregort
Fine four-legged character
A toy stuck on with chewing gum
Your dinosaur protector

And if I'm ever in a bind
I know you will come through
If experience tells me anything
Fucking shit up is what you do
(in a good way)

Wildfire

Once when I was in primary school
We had a sub teacher who always wore cool
Funky sweaters while she was in class
I always enjoyed it, then this came to pass

While she was in class on a wintry day
The old heater was on, and like any weekday
She stood in front of it, hogging the warmth
When out from behind her, some smoke wisped forth

We tried to yell out but she wasn't having it
While more smoke is coming out from her cable-knit
She told us "be quiet!" till question time started
Tried putting a hand up; my question was darted

Watching on in horror as the smoke just got bigger
She still hasn't noticed, talking 'bout some maths figure
Eventually, I had to yell out "You're on fire!"
She screams, puts it out, and says

"Why the hell didn't you tell me before? I could have died, you know! You can't trust anyone these days, that's for sure"

That was dire!

Pepper

By your perspective
I've known you forever
Related in name and emotion
A day brightened by your existence

A celebrity when you walk the street
Those who don't know you
Want to know you
And I am thankful you are mine

A coat unrivalled by dogs abound
The best to bury a face in
Or roll alongside on cool tiles
Smiling with a gorgeous grin

Tufts between the toes
Ears softer than merino
Going grey like an old man
With the enthusiasm of youth

Though the years tick on
I wouldn't trade our time together
For the inevitable grief
From an untimely separation

A Simple Rickroll

Navigate to the search bar and search for "Never Gonna Give You Up" by Rick Astley
Choose "Never Gonna Give You Up" by Rick Astley from the list of search results
Open the song player and add the song to your playlist "Sexy Jams"
Share the song with your friend Natasha via Messenger.

www.ingramcontent.com/pod-product-compliance
Lightning Source LLC
Chambersburg PA
CBHW051717130826
49812CB00034B/1233
9789357445313